REVISED

The churchwarden's handbook

a practical guide

Ian Russell

kevin mayhew

First published in 2000 by

Kevin Mayhew Ltd
Buxhall, Stowmarket, Suffolk IP14 3BW
Tel: +44 (0) 1449 737978 Fax: +44 (0) 1449 737834
E-mail: info@kevinmayhewltd.com

www.kevinmayhew.com

ISBN 978 1 84003 534 6
Catalogue No. 1500347

Edited by Helen Elliot
Cover design by Jonathan Stroulger

Printed and bound in Great Britain

Contents

About the Author

The Venerable Ian Russell was Archdeacon of Coventry from 1989 to 2000 and has considerable personal experience of working with churchwardens in both rural and urban parishes. He served on the General Synod Working Party on Lay Office Holders in the Church of England, and was on the steering committee involved in revising the legislation which is encapsulated in the Churchwardens Measure 2001. He has also taken an active role in training sessions for wardens within the Diocese of Coventry.

FOREWORD

The office of churchwarden is an ancient one, and has always been a significant task. By the thirteenth century it was already legally recognised. Historically the business and financial side of parochial activity and especially the care of the fabric and furnishings of the church have been uppermost among the responsibilities. Until parochial church councils were established in 1921, churchwardens were the sole official representatives of the laity in each parish.

Since that time the office has continued to develop. Some tasks are now shared with other groups and individuals in the life of the Church, and further duties have been added. All this means that in these days to be a churchwarden is to hold a post of considerable responsibility.

This book seeks to provide information of a non-technical nature to enable those who are already in office to grasp more fully what that involves. It is also designed to help those who have been invited to consider nomination to see more clearly what might lie ahead of them, should they feel it right to accept. Experience suggests that churchwardens are not alone in being asked to consider office within the Church without at the same time being given any clear indication of what is involved. In God's call to us, as his people, we are accountable for those things which are entrusted to us. My prayer is that this book will help that process.

What is written reflects the legal requirements of the Churchwardens Measure 2001, which introduces practices different from those that have been the norm for many years. This book is a response to the requests, made during debate of that Measure in the Church of England

General Synod, for assistance to be available to all those involved in the fulfilment of its obligations.

Although the focus is on the task of the churchwarden, the book is intended also to be of assistance to those elected or chosen as deputy churchwardens. The choice of such a person is allowed for, both under the Church Representation Rules and under a Pastoral Scheme or Bishop's Instrument permitted under the Pastoral Measure 1983. To the deputy the churchwardens may, by a scheme approved by the annual meeting, delegate some of their functions.

A number of churchwardens and deputy churchwardens in the Archdeaconry of Coventry assisted me by reading the script and making suggestions for its improvement. I am grateful to them for their assistance. I am grateful also for the help of Mrs Angela Skelton, who prepared the script for the publishers. In addition I express my sincere appreciation to Miss Ingrid Slaughter, the General Synod Assistant Legal Adviser. She has been willing to check the legal accuracy of the document as well as to suggest items for inclusion, which I may have otherwise omitted. Nevertheless the responsibility for what is written in the pages that follow is mine alone. It is dedicated to all who offer their time, their abilities and themselves to Christ as churchwardens in the life of his Church.

Ian Russell

A CHURCHWARDEN'S PRAYER

Eternal God,
when you call your servants to a task,
you promise to give them grace
and strength to accomplish it.
Mercifully look upon those
who have special responsibilities
in your Church as churchwardens,
that, beginning their work in reverence,
following it through with obedience
and completing it in faithful devotion,
they may be renewed by your Holy Spirit
to live in constant thankfulness to you;
through Jesus Christ our Redeemer.

Amen.

Chapter 1
THE QUALITIES NEEDED

A churchwarden is involved in leadership in the life of the local Church. This requires three particular qualities, of which the first is a willingness to acknowledge that leadership within the Church is in response to God's call to us and he equips us for the task. In these respects we depend upon his grace. The second is the realisation that, if God does call us to serve him in this way, it is not for our own benefit but for the service of others, for the building up of his Church and to his glory. The third essential is to remember at all times that those who hold lay office have an obligation to collaborate with other lay and ordained people in order that the responsibilities of church life may be properly fulfilled. Leadership is not simply something which we fulfil ourselves. It is something that we share with others.

Three-way task

In the life of a parish the churchwarden has the dual role of representing the laity and also working closely with the minister. On occasions either one of these can represent an unenviable task. How, for example, do you represent the laity as a whole when there appears such a lack of common ground between what may be described as the traditional and the innovative approaches to worship, or between those who appear to be urging the Church to move forward in quite differing ways? Yet, despite such situations, the churchwarden is a vital lay leader in the parish and needs to represent the lay viewpoint.

At the same time there is also the responsibility to work with the minister. Later in the book further consideration will be given to how this can be done creatively and positively. Suffice it at this point to suggest that unless there is a willingness to discharge this duty, then the reasons for accepting nomination must be questioned. For someone to seek this post in order to oppose or to frustrate the purposes of the minister is certainly not the right motivation.

The churchwarden is also a bishop's officer, and as such both responsible and accountable to the bishop. Consequently the person appointed needs to bear in mind that the role has a wider significance than just within the parish alone.

Example to others

A churchwarden – as any other leader within the Church – is to be an example of Christian faith and life. Such must be demonstrated in both word and deed. Others must be helped to progress in their Christian discipleship by the words and deeds of the churchwardens. It is part and parcel of the churchwarden's job to help the local Church to be obedient to the will of God.

The ways in which this happens differ greatly from one person to another, from one place to another. As a rule a churchwarden should be regularly involved in the worshipping congregation of the parish, and demonstrate a readiness to 'go the extra mile' as an indication of a Christian commitment. Hence the statutory requirement for the choice to be made from those who have been baptised, are on the church electoral roll of the parish, and are regular communicants.

The diocesan bishop, though able to do so in exceptional cases, should only infrequently need to permit someone not satisfying the requirements regarding entry on the electoral roll or communicant status to be nominated. As regards the age at which a person may become a churchwarden, the requirement is that a person be 21 years of age. Whilst it is recognised that a person can be a member of a parochial church council [PCC] at 16 and a charity trustee at 18, the minimum age for a churchwarden of 21 acknowledges the highly responsible nature of the office, and the demands of time, effort and Christian experience required. It is also a post that can, as has already been hinted at, require significant maturity. Again in exceptional circumstances the bishop could permit someone to be nominated at a younger age.

Being a churchwarden demands considerable time and energy; demands which, while being almost inevitable, may also sometimes be added to by the expectations of other members of the Church. The nature of the responsibility is such that someone whose gifts include being moderately well organised and businesslike will have a distinct advantage, but factors of this nature should not be overstated, especially since their importance diminishes as experience is gained. Nonetheless, candidates for the post and those who choose them need realistically to be aware of the likely burdens. Counting the cost and a sober judgement of capability have their rightful place in the consideration of an appropriate nominee.

In all cases the requirement is now that any candidate willing to be chosen should signify in writing their readiness to serve. Gone are the days when people could be nominated without themselves giving assent.

Disqualifications

Sadly, there are also grounds which would disqualify a person from being nominated. Just as someone cannot now be a PCC member if they are disqualified under Section 72(i) of the Charities Act 1993 so, unless a waiver has been granted by the Charity Commissioners, such a person cannot be a churchwarden. Since the position involves the handling of money and the ownership and care of valuable property, total financial integrity is called for.

Similarly, any person convicted of an offence covered by Schedule 1 of the Children and Young Persons Act 1933 would be disqualified, both to protect the interests of parents and their children, and for the sake of the individual concerned. Those with a tendency to child abuse are often faced with very severe temptation to re-offend, even if a long period has elapsed since any former incident. Grave scandal also needs to be avoided.

The aim should be to find candidates of transparent sincerity, manifest integrity and Christian commitment. Everything that can be done should be done to ensure that those chosen meet these vital criteria.

Chapter 2
HOW THE CHOICE IS MADE

In many parishes there is general acceptance of the principle of lay ministry, and the importance of all members of the congregation being actively involved in the worship, life and mission of the Church. Care always needs to be taken to ensure that unreasonable demands are not made of anybody, and one means to this end is to provide opportunities for training for the increasing variety of lay ministries. As far as actual, or potential, churchwardens are concerned, this will often be best done within a deanery, archdeaconry or diocese.

Such training will help both those who might become churchwardens and those who choose the potential candidates. At the same time it is important to ensure that people are encouraged to offer their particular gifts and to fulfil the task in their particular way, without simply reproducing what might have been seen in others.

Possible candidates
Because of the nature of the office it is necessary for both the minister and the laity to be involved in approaching nominees, though the actual nomination is solely in the hands of those entitled to attend the annual meeting of the parishioners, which has to be held not later than 30 April in each year, and which often precedes the Annual Parochial Church Meeting.

Churchwardens are chosen annually and serve for a year at a time. Candidates have to be nominated and seconded in writing, and have to sign a statement that they are both willing to serve and are not disqualified from doing so. All such nominations, and the accompanying consents, have to be made to the minister of the parish before the meeting of the parishioners commences.

In order to comply with these requirements, and in recognition of the significance of the office, careful and prayerful thought and action needs to be taken.

Number of churchwardens

There should be two churchwardens for every parish. Where one parish includes more than one parish church or parish centre of worship (legally designated) under the Pastoral Measure, two churchwardens are to be chosen for each building. All are churchwardens of the whole parish, with responsibility for the whole, unless there is some arrangement by which separate duties are arranged in respect of a particular building.

Whilst it may be difficult in some places to find two suitable people willing to serve, every effort should be made to do so. The duties are such that the burden on one person can be immense. If in the end only one or even no churchwarden is found, the help of the archdeacon should be sought as to ways forward in that situation.

It is not permitted for a person to be churchwarden of more than one parish at any one time, unless the parishes concerned are within the same benefice or benefice held in plurality, or are served by the same minister.

The meeting of the parishioners

The churchwardens are elected by a meeting of those whose names are on the church electoral roll of the parish and those who are resident within the parish and registered as local government electors. The election is conducted in the same way as for the election of members of the parochial church council under the Church Representation Rules. It is not possible for churchwardens to be elected by the 'single transferable vote' system.

As has been indicated, every effort should be made by the minister and the parishioners to agree on the nominations. In some instances, however, the minister of the parish may feel that the election of a particular nominee might give rise to serious difficulties in the fulfilment of their respective tasks. If that be the case the minister may state, before the election is held, that he or she will appoint one person from among those already nominated. Having named that person, an election is then held to enable the meeting to choose the other churchwarden.

Length of service

A churchwarden is elected to serve until the next meeting of parishioners, and that person's service is limited to six successive periods of office. This is designed to help those who are willing to serve but who wish to do so for a limited period. Equally it is to assist in those places where there are several suitable candidates, so that each is given the opportunity of bringing their particular gifts to the office, should they be chosen.

Although this is a legal requirement, it can be overridden at any time by a resolution taken by a meeting of the parishioners if they decide that it is not appropriate in their situation. If such a resolution is carried, it may subsequently be revoked at a later date. Obviously it is necessary, should such a resolution be moved at a meeting of parishioners, that this is done prior to the election of the churchwardens. In this way candidates and electors alike are fully aware of the position.

Swearing-in

Once chosen as churchwarden, that person does not legally take up their appointment until they have opportunity publicly to declare their readiness to discharge their responsibilities and to make a written declaration confirming this and stating that they are not disqualified. This itself is part of the process sometimes known as 'swearing-in'.

Such opportunity is given each year on a date not later than 31 July. The responsibility for arranging this lies with the diocesan bishop, and is frequently delegated by him to the archdeacon. In the normal course of events the 'swearing-in' and 'admission' is part of the 'archdeacon's visitation', usually held annually. This gives an opportunity for churchwardens to meet with each other in corporate worship and to consider together aspects of their office in their particular parochial situations.

If for any reason a person chosen as a churchwarden is not able to attend on the date given, arrangements have to be made to ensure that they are admitted before 31 July. If this does not happen, a casual vacancy is created, and a further meeting of parishioners has to be convened in accordance with the procedure laid down for any casual vacancy arising in a churchwarden's office.

Once a churchwarden has been admitted, that person becomes an officer of the bishop. This means that the warden concerned conducts the bishop on any occasion when he shares in the worship of the parish church. This involves carrying a churchwarden's staff and leading the bishop to his place. It also implies a readiness to share with the bishop any situation that gives rise to serious concern in the life of the parish. This can be done by a direct approach to the bishop or by informal discussion with the archdeacon. Being officers of the bishop also means churchwardens are to respond to any request made for information regarding their parish.

In summary, the title of bishop's officer underlines the importance of the office of churchwarden and the consequent careful approach that must be taken in finding suitable candidates.

Chapter 3
WORKING WITH THE MINISTER

According to Canon E1*, a churchwarden 'shall be foremost in representing the laity and in co-operating with the incumbent'. From this standpoint it could be said that the churchwardens are the leading lay people in the parish and, as such, share with the minister in the leadership of the parish. As a result they, churchwardens and minister alike, co-operate in the whole mission of the Church, pastoral, evangelistic, social and ecumenical.

Co-operation

What is necessary to facilitate such co-operation? One answer is that those concerned make every effort to get to know each other as individuals. Friendship is crucial. So also is a willingness to give time to co-operation. There should be regular opportunities to meet and discuss things in an atmosphere and setting of prayer. Certainly the standing committee of the PCC will be one such opportunity, but other opportunities should be made when concerns can be shared openly and honestly. It would seem preferable that these occasions should be face-to-face meetings, but a telephone call is also a valuable means of keeping up-to-date. It is also amazing how much can be shared following a Sunday service, when there is a will to do so!

As has already been indicated, if there is likely to be a problem with this kind of mutual co-operation then special care needs to be taken. For example, should it appear that the nomination of a particular person as churchwarden might give rise to serious difficulties between them, then the minister is free to appoint one

* See Appendix, page 47

churchwarden from among the persons nominated, with the meeting electing the other churchwarden. In such a situation all the parties concerned should be prepared to make extra efforts to co-operate.

As far as a potential churchwarden is concerned, if there is an unwillingness even to attempt to co-operate then their motive for agreeing to nomination must be in question. It cannot be right for someone to be chosen as churchwarden whose aim in their period of office is to thwart the minister in his or her ministry. As Canon E1 powerfully states, churchwardens are 'to use their best endeavours by example and precept to encourage the parishioners in the practice of true religion and to promote unity and peace among them'. Such encouragement and promotion is never furthered by suspicion, hostility or outright opposition.

Difficult situations

Yet, having said that, there are occasions when a churchwarden, in seeking to represent the laity, does not find it at all easy to co-operate with the incumbent. What happens when, having taken soundings among the laity in relation to a particular suggestion about some change in the life of the Church, the churchwarden feels bound to oppose the minister? It is impractical to try to answer this in a way that would meet every situation, and it is impossible to please everyone. But we are not bound to do so. We are bound first to seek to discover and follow the will of God. We are bound to seek to do his will in Christian love – and such love will, at times, require all concerned to take more time to consider and to pray than might come naturally to them. We are bound, even in situations where a way forward is undertaken which is not of our choosing, to seek to discern whether God is using that to achieve his purpose in ways that we might never have imagined possible.

Bridging the gap

In this whole area of co-operation a churchwarden sometimes has another role, namely to seek to re-present to the laity the aims and purpose of the minister. If the minister is fulfilling his or her part in their mutual relationship, a churchwarden will often have a deeper understanding of the thinking of the minister than most other people in the parish. It is immensely helpful when this is shared appropriately with others by the churchwarden. In a sense, a churchwarden is a bridge. Not just the minister's 'yes' person but, on the basis of a desire to co-operate with the minister, someone who is prepared to ensure that his or her 'mind' is passed on to a wider group of people.

Another vital way of supporting the minister is to see that undue administrative and other burdens are not placed on him or her. In many instances, responsibility for matters of insurance, heating, cleaning, the maintenance of the church and other parochial buildings, and preparing the church for funerals, can all readily be undertaken by members of the congregation. Similarly a concern for the repair or replacement of items such as kneelers, service books, bells, noticeboards and the like can well be a shared responsibility, allowing others to offer their skills and expertise to the life of the church.

Pastoral care

A further aspect of this co-operation is that the churchwarden should be foremost in caring pastorally for the minister. Ensuring that his or her expenses of office are fully met is one area of this care. Clergy stipend levels are fixed on the assumption that parochial expenses will be reimbursed in full. Those whose working expenses are not reimbursed are receiving less than their full stipend because part of the stipend they receive is being used to pay their working expenses. Churchwardens should make sure that their minister does claim legitimate working expenses – determined according to guidance given by the Archbishop's Council, and agreed at least by the parish standing committee.

Other aspects of pastoral care which need to be remembered include ensuring the minister has regular time off and annual holidays, and offering hospitality when a new minister arrives and on frequent occasions afterwards. Further examples might be encouraging people to rally round in times of ill-health, for this, as with holidays, might mean that there is no minister available in the parish. In such an event the churchwardens will need to be fully in touch with the situation and be ready to take whatever action is required in the circumstances. Particular occasions of joy or sadness which the minister, or his or her family might experience, should also evoke sensitive and appropriate response. Indeed a whole range of practical gestures of friendship and generosity, even including the offering of tickets for a concert, the theatre or a sporting occasion, are possible.

All these are examples of care – simply wanting to befriend and support – and are a part of what working with the minister can mean when interpreted positively and imaginatively.

Chapter 4
WORKING WITH OTHERS

Anyone chosen as a churchwarden will find themselves sharing the job with a co-warden. More often than not this person will have served for at least a year. This does not mean that the person newly chosen is to be seen as 'junior' to a 'senior' warden. The nature of the relationship is a partnership. The quality of the relationship should itself set an example to others of good and positive co-working in the Body of Christ.

From this point of view it is important that churchwardens take the trouble to get to know each other. As with other cases in the life of the Christian Church, they will not necessarily have themselves chosen to share the church wardenship with each other. But they now have that joint responsibility. Neither of them will on their own be capable of performing all the duties, and they should not aim to do so. Responsibilities can be shared according to interests and abilities. This kind of partnership is bound, at some point, to require patience, understanding and forbearance – as does any partnership.

Assistance

In some parishes churchwardens find it useful to have someone to assist them. Such a person is selected by the Annual Parochial Church Meeting, the church council or the wardens themselves. Two things need to be noted in this context: first, that when churchwardens are admitted to office, theirs and theirs alone is the legal responsibility of fulfilling that office. Only in cases where a parish has two or more places of worship, including a team ministry, can there be any legal powers to delegate tasks. Secondly, whilst the opportunity to delegate is limited, the opportunity to seek assistance from others is unlimited.

In this respect, as from the point of view of accuracy of title, someone chosen to assist the churchwardens in any way is best seen as an assistant warden. It is certainly possible under Canon E2* for a sidesman to act in this way. The decision as to how this practice is worked out is best decided locally. In many places sidesmen will assist churchwardens in their responsibility for the seating of the congregation in the church and for the maintenance of good order and behaviour. Churchwardens should arrange the sidesmen's rota and ensure that sidesmen know what their duties are. In this respect churchwardens have the overall responsibility for the preparation of the church for worship and for ensuring that the particular books and any other material required are available so that those who attend are able to take a full part in the worship.

Money

The churchwardens are responsible for the way in which the financial offerings of the people, normally called the collection, are made, and must ensure that the money collected is dealt with responsibly. This includes its careful counting after the service, preferably by at least two people, and accurate recording of all amounts contained in any specially provided envelopes. All totals, from whatever source, should be itemised in the service register. Special care should be taken as to the monies kept in the church safe. It is preferable for proceeds from Sunday collections to be put into a bank night safe in order to prevent large amounts being kept in the church safe overnight. Steps should be taken to ensure that the church treasurer is fully aware of all procedures for the

* See Appendix, page 49

recording, safe keeping and banking of all money received. It cannot be stressed too strongly that public money has to be dealt with according to the highest standards. A responsible stewardship is vital both in the giving of money and in the ways in which it is handled.

The bishop

A churchwarden is a bishop's officer and something of the significance of that title has already been stated. In addition, as a bishop's officer, should a churchwarden wish to resign during the course of their period of service they have to do so directly to the bishop. This means that they have to write to the bishop giving notice of intention to resign. Provided the date of the resignation is two months from the giving of the notice, the bishop has to accept it. Alternatively he may agree to an earlier date, after consulting with the minister and any other churchwarden of the parish.

Since a churchwarden serves for only one year at a time the number of occasions when someone resigns are relatively few. There are, nevertheless, situations in which a person might, voluntarily or otherwise, vacate the office. One such would be if they were to move house; another, if they were to become legally disqualified from holding office. A further alternative would be for them not to sign the statement of willingness to serve as churchwarden for a further year, thus rendering themselves ineligible for nomination at the ensuing meeting of parishioners.

The archdeacon

More often than not the bishop will invite the archdeacon to substitute for him in admitting churchwardens to office. This gives the archdeacon a special responsibility for all churchwardens which will be fulfilled in a variety of ways, but prayer, support and a readiness to give any advice requested will certainly be essential.

The admission of churchwardens is often carried out as part of the annual visitation of the archdeacon, and happens in various stages. The first stage is the sending of the Articles of Inquiry to the churchwardens in the early part of the year. These will be designed to discover certain information about the parish and the life of the church. Churchwardens have a duty to complete these Articles. They are one of the means by which they give an account of ways in which they have fulfilled their task.

The Articles will usually have to be returned to the archdeacon before the visitation services, which are normally held in May or June, as soon as possible after churchwardens are chosen. As has already been indicated, a churchwarden, though chosen at an earlier date, is not in law reckoned to be a churchwarden until he or she has been admitted. So, at a visitation service, where there has been a change of churchwarden, both the retiring warden and the newly chosen person should be present. The first will be there to mark the completion of their responsibility. The second will be there to offer themselves to God for the responsibility for which they have been chosen.

During a visitation the archdeacon may follow the practice of meeting with churchwardens privately, or at least he will meet churchwardens personally, and they will have the opportunity to meet and talk with each other.

The registrar

Each diocese has a registrar who receives an annual retainer to provide legal advice, within certain limits, to a wide range of office holders in the diocese. Churchwardens should feel able to consult the diocesan registrar on any legal matter that properly arises in connection with their duties or official business. Indeed, if legal advice is needed, churchwardens are encouraged to seek such advice sooner rather than later.

The rural/area dean
Churchwardens will also have to work with their rural/ area dean. In some cases he or she will be the first port of call for information or help, since the rural/area dean is not seen as an authority figure in quite the way that the bishop or the archdeacon might be.

Rural/area deans will frequently have contact with churchwardens when acting on behalf of the archdeacon. This might happen when churchwardens are being admitted, or more likely when the rural/area dean is visiting for the parish inspection, which is required at least once every three years. Such visits will involve the checking of the terrier and inventory, and, probably, the logbook, parish registers and records, and an inspection of the church and churchyard.

The churchwardens will work most closely with the rural/area dean when the parish is in an interregnum/ vacancy. But this is such an important period for the life of a parish that more detailed information is given in Chapter 6.

Whatever the circumstances of the contact, the rural/ area dean, like the archdeacon, is to be thought of as someone who is available for consultation at any time. The churchwardens' ability and willingness to achieve good working relationships with the rural dean, the archdeacon and the bishop can serve as examples of the way in which Christians are enabled to work together in church leadership and are strengthened in so doing.

Chapter 5
WORKING WITH THE PAROCHIAL CHURCH COUNCIL

As a result of the Churchwardens Measure it will only be in exceptional cases that a churchwarden is not a member of the parochial church council (PCC). Indeed such membership begins from the date when they are chosen, although they will only later be admitted to office. Churchwardens have a particularly important task as members of the PCC in that it is the PCC which, in law, has responsibility for the financial affairs of the church; the care, maintenance, preservation and insurance of the fabric, goods and ornaments of the church; and the care and maintenance of the churchyard. These responsibilities combine with concern for the ongoing worship and mission of the church. In other words, PCC members have power to make decisions which affect most areas of church life. It is right that all matters of general importance be discussed by the minister and the PCC members together.

Although the PCC elects a vice-chairman this is not a responsibility that will necessarily come to one of the churchwardens. They will however be ex-officio members of the standing committee. Should the PCC fail to appoint someone to act as treasurer, the churchwardens may also have to undertake this responsibility.

Inventory and terrier

The churchwardens are legal owners, on behalf of the parishioners, of the plate, ornaments, movable furniture and furnishings and all other articles belonging to the church. As such they have to ensure, in consultation with the minister, that an inventory of all articles belonging to each church in their care is compiled and kept up to date. They have the same duty in relation to the terrier of the lands belonging to the church. This is very important. On taking up office, a churchwarden should check the inventory and terrier. He or she should then sign, along with the outgoing warden, to certify that this check has been made and that the contents are accurate. A copy of the inventory should be sent to the person designated by the bishop. Alterations should also be notified on a regular basis.

Logbook

Along with the terrier and inventory, churchwardens also have to maintain a logbook which details all work done to the church, its articles and lands, with relevant papers. This again must be done in consultation with the minister. In recent years the production of a loose-leaf format for the logbook, as well as the inventory and terrier, has made easier the job of compiling and of keeping them up to date. It also makes reproducing information more straightforward.

Under the Care of Churches and Ecclesiastical Jurisdiction Measure, 1991, the churchwardens have also:

(a) to ensure that the fabric of the church and all articles belonging to it are inspected at least every calendar year. Such an inspection might best be done in the early part of the year. The wardens themselves are not required personally to do the inspection but they are required to ensure it is done. This may be carried out by the PCC fabric officer or members of the fabric committee. Such an arrangement ensures that if the wardens do not wish to do this personally then someone within the PCC or congregation is available who is happy to undertake the task. Whatever the arrangement arrived at, the wardens should be closely associated with it.

(b) to produce to the PCC the terrier, inventory and log-book covering the previous year. These must first be checked by the churchwardens, in consultation with the minister. A signed statement that the contents are accurate should accompany their presentation to the PCC. It is important that such action on the part of the churchwardens is matched by PCC members showing real concern and interest, as part of the responsibility they share in respect of the care, maintenance and preservation of the fabric, goods and ornaments of the church.

(c) to make an annual fabric report to the PCC. This report is to cover work done during the previous year and should focus in particular on action taken or proposed to implement the recommendations of the latest quinquennial report (see below). The fabric report should be presented to the PCC at the meeting before the Annual Parochial Church Meeting and is then open for discussion and amendment by the PCC.

(d) to present this considered report, preferably in a written form, to the Annual Parochial Church Meeting. This enables those on the electoral roll of the church to be kept fully informed about the situation regarding the fabric and contents of their church building. In addition a copy of this fabric report may be sent to the archdeacon and to the inspecting architect so that each can be kept in the picture about ways in which the recommendations of the latest quinquennial report on the church are being implemented.

Quinquennial inspection

Each church covered by the Inspection of Churches Measure, 1955, is required to be inspected every five years by an authorised architect or surveyor. Their report will set out items needing attention and will be arranged in order of priority. Although the churchwardens do not have sole responsibility for the consideration of these recommendations they should certainly assist the PCC to establish repair priorities for the next five years.

The work itself, although recommended in the report, cannot begin until such time as a 'faculty' is granted to enable the necessary action to be taken. An application for a faculty is normally made in the name of the minister and churchwardens. Such an application will include a specification detailing the work for which permission is sought as well as a clear indication as to how it will be funded. Since this faculty procedure does not apply in the case of some minor works, it is a wise precaution for the churchwardens to check the guidance given by the chancellor of the diocese as to whether permission is required or not in any specific instance.

It is also worth remembering that, even though churches are covered by faculty jurisdiction in relation to work on the building, it may also be necessary for planning permission to be sought from the local authority in order to carry out certain items of work. This would, for example, include additions to, and work which affects, the external appearance of the building.

Whilst the recommendations of a quinquennial report can involve a PCC having to raise significant funds, major expenditure can be avoided in some instances by ensuring that routine maintenance is carried out. Defects attended to quickly, gutters cleared regularly, slipped slates or tiles repositioned and the base of walls kept dry and free from vegetation will save much heartache and cost at a later date. A churchwarden does not have to do all these things personally but should make sure that they are done.

The continuing responsibility for the fabric and furnishings of church buildings is a very considerable one in these days. Many of our churches are an important part of our national heritage, having been carefully and lovingly maintained over many years. There is therefore a delicate balance to be held between meeting the worshipping and mission needs of the current congregation and respecting the concerns of those for whom conservation issues are vital.

The churchyard

The duties of the churchwardens with regard to the care and maintenance of the churchyard are again carried out on behalf of the PCC. Whilst churchyards are also subject to faculty jurisdiction, there may be instances, as for example where trees are protected by a Tree Preservation Order or because they are in a conservation area, where an approach has to be made to the local authority. In such matters, as in all cases where the requirements of the law are to be met, the churchwardens, as officers of the bishop, have an interest and a concern. In many instances the PCC will look to the churchwardens for guidance and therefore some basic knowledge of these matters is valuable.

Security

This is an increasingly important issue for churchwardens. Generally speaking, members of a congregation often know little about the value of some of the articles which are in frequent use in the church. The market value, for example, of an ancient bishop's chair or a brass lectern both make insurance cover vital and require that every reasonable care be taken to prevent theft or vandalism.

Church plate and ornaments should be carefully photographed, with full details of dimensions, weight, any inscriptions and the significance of hallmarks included in the inventory. Church plate should be locked in the church safe immediately after use. Portable items should be security marked. The vestry windows and doors should be made secure.

In some places alarm systems, video security cameras or some type of church watch programme may be appropriate. Again, the churchwardens have to be involved since they are the legal owners of the articles within the church on behalf of the parishioners.

Chapter 6
DURING A VACANCY

If the churchwardens feel that there is a lot to do when a minister is in post, their ideas are sometimes changed when an interregnum/vacancy occurs! Different dioceses adopt different practices but, whatever happens, under the Church of England (Miscellaneous Provisions) Measure 1992, the churchwardens will be appointed as sequestrators unless, in a team ministry, a team vicar is appointed. This responsibility for the running of the parish will be a shared one, involving probably the rural/area dean and others. One beneficial effect of this arrangement is that churchwardens, if appointed, know that there is someone else who, on the basis of greater experience, is able to advise them.

Bearing in mind different approaches, it is probable that a diocese will offer sequestrators written guidance, and such notes will be given to them before the vacancy actually begins. Being able to consider their duties at an early stage gives churchwardens a good opportunity to prepare for them more carefully than would otherwise be the case.

In a situation where there are clergy licensed by the bishop to serve in the parish, for example a team vicar, an assistant curate or an ordained local minister, there is sometimes a temptation to imagine that they are responsible for the parish. In law this is not the case, though in a team ministry a team vicar might be appointed as acting team rector and/or a sequestrator. Generally speaking it is the sequestrators who have the responsibility for every aspect of the life of the parish, whether it be Sunday services, occasional offices, pastoral care or undertaking mission in and to the area. In practice this should not mean that churchwardens appear to 'take over' these things. Where people already have responsibility, they should be encouraged to continue to fulfil it. This applies to the clergy as to the laity. A curate, for example, will be of immense assistance in many aspects of the life of the parish during a vacancy but he or she does not have the right to chair the PCC. That becomes the task of the elected vice-chairman. Indeed, in many instances an interregnum, following the initial 'bereavement' period, can become a time when people work together fruitfully, knowing that if the Church is to move forward they have a vital part to play in the process. The churchwardens' job is to encourage and support all involved.

Occasionally the bishop will give a member of the clergy a temporary responsibility during an interregnum as a consultant. This is not seen as a leadership role but rather as helping the parish or team to take stock of itself, to reconsider what its priorities should be and to work out what steps to take to make these objectives possible.

Providing for services

One of the earliest questions to be faced in an interregnum is whether it is reasonable to maintain the existing pattern of services. The availability of people ready and able to conduct services will be a prime consideration. When a decision has been made, a rota can be drawn up. It is good to be able to work two to three months in advance, and perhaps more if the month of August is included. The outgoing minister can be a great help in getting cover, certainly up until the date of his or her taking up a new post, resigning or retiring.

It is one thing to arrange for people to take services but it is also essential to ensure that they know what is expected of them. It is too easy to imagine that all visitors will automatically know the form of service, the readings, the music and any special peculiarities of the church.

A telephone call a week before they are due to come is a help both to the visitor and to the churchwarden.

If a visitor is to conduct a baptism, marriage or funeral service, careful thought needs to be given as to who will make the necessary preparations beforehand. Responsibility for this should preferably rest with the parish, but it is important that the officiating minister is fully briefed well before the event as to the content of such preparation. When they have taken a service, the churchwardens should offer the payment of travelling expenses to the minister concerned. Such amounts are paid from the PCC account.

Just occasionally, despite the most carefully laid plans, a visitor may not arrive in time or even at all for a service. A churchwarden has the authority to lead a non-eucharistic act of worship and in such a situation the opportunity occurs to do so. Sometimes such a service is the best remembered of the whole interregnum, and enables the churchwarden to discover previously unsuspected gifts!

Where a benefice is vacant churchwardens have the authority to arrange for a suitable lay person to lead the worship at morning or evening prayer (except for pronouncing the absolution).

Fees

Details of any fees, to whom they are to be paid and how this is to be done, will be contained in the diocesan instructions to sequestrators. Such payments will be made from the income received from the marriage, funeral and other fees that would have been paid to the minister if there had been one. (During a vacancy in the benefice, the fee which would normally go to the incumbent must be paid to the Diocesan Board of Finance in accordance with directions given by the Board after consulting the bishop.

The first step must therefore be to make arrangements with the secretary of the Diocesan Board of Finance as to how the fees are to be dealt with during the particular vacancy.) If such payments are insufficient to pay visiting ministers then those costs are paid from the Diocesan Stipends Fund. This applies also in relation to any expenses incurred by the rural/area dean, the churchwardens or others in their capacity as sequestrators. Obviously, during a vacancy, any parochial expenses met by the churchwardens in the fulfilment of their responsibilities should, as when there is a minister in post, be paid from the PCC account.

The care of the parsonage
As sequestrators, churchwardens should make proper arrangements for the security of the parsonage house during a vacancy. The diocesan bishop has various rights and powers over the house during this period, and he will probably authorise the Diocesan Parsonages Committee to fulfil his responsibility. In the local situation the sequestrators have the duty to supervise the care of the house and to ensure that services such as gas, electricity and water are controlled. Sadly, steps will often have to be taken to protect the house against vandalism. Many of these tasks can be fulfilled by frequent visits to the property.

In some instances the house may be let during a vacancy, according to diocesan policy. Care must be taken in such instances not to intrude upon the privacy of the occupants and so careful practical arrangements have to be made in relation to matters like post and telephone. In the event of the house, whether it is let or not, accommodating parish equipment such as a photocopier, issues of security and access need to be agreed. Even if the house is unoccupied, there is no automatic right for the PCC to use the house. Where this is desired, permission has first to be obtained.

In such matters the diocesan secretary or the person responsible for parsonage houses in the diocese is always willing to give advice.

The new appointment

The length of any particular vacancy is unpredictable. But what is certain is that the requirements of the Patronage (Benefices) Measure 1986 mean that the wardens and the PCC will be intimately involved in the process of making a new appointment.

Whilst the outworking of the provisions of the Measure may vary from diocese to diocese, it is the duty of the PCC to prepare a statement describing the conditions, needs and traditions of the parish. As much information as possible should be provided to give a comprehensive picture of the parish. Since the document becomes a public document when completed, some of those who read it will have no means of knowing about the parish except through the information it contains.

This statement will conclude with setting out ideas for any potential developments or new pastoral or other opportunities envisaged. In the light of these factors the PCC will then state the qualities and attributes they would wish to see in their new minister.

The parish representatives

The PCC also has the further major responsibility of electing two lay members of the council to act as its representatives in connection with the selection of a new minister. Anyone chosen should be in a position to become actively involved in the ongoing process. The crucial factor in this vital choice must be identifying those who are the most suitable persons for the task. Whilst either or both of the churchwardens may be chosen, it is equally possible that neither will be. The circumstances in each situation will differ. Should the PCC fail to appoint any representative, the two churchwardens will then act in this capacity, unless one of them is the presenting patron or their representative. If therefore, just one churchwarden is qualified to act, that person acts as the sole representative of the parish. It is obviously preferable, should the PCC want the churchwardens to be its representatives, that it positively elect them to act, rather than that they be appointed by default.

As the process continues it is possible that what is called the 'Section 12' meeting may be held at the request of the PCC, the presenting patron or their representative, or of the bishop. If such a meeting is held it chooses its own chairman; it is probably appropriate for the chairman to be someone other than the patron, the bishop or one of the PCC representatives. One of the churchwardens or the PCC vice-chairman, if either one has not been chosen as a PCC representative, would seem to be a strong candidate for the job. The business of such a Section 12 meeting is to provide a forum for an exchange of views on the PCC statement, and to consider a statement made by the bishop as to the needs of the diocese and the wider Church. The churchwardens' experience of the parish is likely to be of great value in such a mutual sharing of information and concerns.

Should neither of the churchwardens be a PCC representative, they may feel excluded from the selection process as it continues, especially as any candidate invited by the patron to consider the vacancy is not obliged, when visiting the parish, to meet anyone other than the PCC representatives. In such a situation the churchwarden is in no different a position from any other member of the PCC or the congregation. Patience and understanding are required until such time as a candidate or candidates ask to meet a wider circle of the congregation. Churchwardens should certainly be among that group, and may well be of immense help in answering particular questions raised by a candidate.

Once the PCC representatives have approved the nominee of the patron and the bishop has given his approval, the patron presents the person to the bishop for admission to the parish. Subject to that agreement, an announcement is made and the date for the institution or collation is fixed.

Suspension of presentation
For the purposes of pastoral reorganisation the bishop may, with the consent of the Diocesan Pastoral Committee and after consultation with the patron, the PCC, the rural/area dean and lay co-chairman of the Deanery, suspend presentation to the benefice. The process then followed in appointing a new minister enables the bishop himself, in effect, to nominate the new minister. Since the bishop is required to consult with the PCC and so far as is practicable, the patron, the process of appointment may be minimally or substantially different from that used in the appointment of an incumbent. The bishop himself makes the actual appointment and he will nominate a new minister to be a priest-in-charge. The service at which that person takes up his or her responsibility is usually called a licensing or a commissioning.

The welcome
At this point the churchwardens will be fully involved. They need to maintain an overview of the arrangements that will have to be made to welcome the new minister. This might involve approval being sought for parochial help in the preparing of the parsonage house. Invitations to the institution, collation or licensing, as the case may be, will need to be prepared and sent out to invited

guests. Preparations for the service will be co-ordinated by the rural/area dean, and a rehearsal held.

Before that special event occurs the new minister will usually move into the house and the churchwardens should be among the first to provide a welcome and help with the settling-in process. Fellowship and assistance offered at such a time will be appreciated and remembered and can provide the basis of a friendship that continues for years. Finally the new minister is instituted or licensed at a service in which the churchwardens have a significant part to play. Of all the laity in that early period, the churchwardens are most crucial. But, as has already been indicated, not only then!

Chapter 7
HANDING ON THE POSITION

Being a churchwarden is quite unlike most positions in the life of the Church – it is for one year only! Anyone having fulfilled the responsibility for that period of time is free, should they so wish, to hand it over to someone else. This can be done simply by not agreeing to nomination for a second time. Someone wanting to follow this course of action at the end of their first or any subsequent year in office should complete with their co-warden the Articles of Inquiry. As has been indicated, this is one of the ways they render account for the way in which they have fulfilled their responsibility. It is hoped that they will attend the Visitation Service, as evidence of their handing on their task to a new warden and in order to pray for him or her as they undertake it.

Questions are sometimes raised about the requirement in the Churchwardens Measure that after six consecutive years of office a churchwarden be disqualified from standing again in the same parish – though a parish may resolve that this should not apply in their case. As has already been said, the reasoning behind this is to give opportunity for several members of the congregation to serve the cause of Christ and his Church as a warden. If one person continues to hold office year after year, their experience and wisdom notwithstanding, the danger is that others are thereby rendered unable or unwilling to stand for election. Since other lay members of the PCC may well have to stand down after a term of years should the Annual Parochial Church Meeting so decide, this principle has now been extended to churchwardens. Of course this is not to say such a person can never be nominated again. It is just to say that a break of at least a year is required before this can happen.

Since the responsibilities of being a churchwarden are so significant, it takes a while to get to grips with all the aspects of the job. Each person will bring their own distinctive contribution to the position, and therefore by adopting this particular requirement in the Measure, a parish can benefit from the gifts of a whole variety of people.

Life afterwards

At the same time, it will mean that there is likely to be a larger group of people who have served as wardens than previously. It is vital that their experience is not lost, but put to good use. Equally they should feel free to offer themselves in Christian service in some other capacity. Service in the cause of Christ is lifelong, and there should be no place for the 'I've done my bit' attitude.

This does not mean that ex-wardens should become a sort of super class of lay people, rather that they should be ready to assist the churchwardens in office in any way they can. Their wisdom is invaluable, so long as they are not convinced that theirs is the only way of fulfilling the task.

Should an outgoing warden nominate his or her successor? This would not seem to be the best approach for fear of denying other members of the congregation their right of nomination or in case other people feel inhibited in putting forward a candidate to oppose the nominee of the outgoing warden. Having said that, there is no reason why the outgoing warden should not be prepared to share something of the nature of the task with anyone who is willing to consider nomination. Far too many wardens have served the Church over the years without being given at the outset any clear idea of what was involved! This booklet was itself written to help ensure that does not happen in the future.

There is life after being a churchwarden. Although, as with many responsibilities, it can be somewhat difficult to adjust, there is often a sense of relief that the duties have been handed on to someone else. There is no reason at all why, in seeking to continue their Christian service, a person who has served as a churchwarden should not remain a member of the PCC if so elected.

Handing over

The time between the meeting of parishioners, when a new warden is chosen, and the date of admission, when that person legally takes on the responsibility, is a crucial period for one warden handing over to another. This period of some weeks is quite invaluable for the two people concerned to get together, and for the newly chosen warden to learn at first hand from his or her predecessor what the position involves. It also gives opportunity for them to check the inventory and terrier together and sign the documents accordingly.

Should a churchwarden decide not to continue in office and no successor is chosen, then the responsibility of the outgoing warden continues until 31 July. After that date a casual vacancy is deemed to have arisen.

Since more people are likely to become wardens in the future, a parish may make one further call on those who have previously served as churchwarden. This is to use their experience to help others see what is involved so that the task does not appear needlessly daunting. If such training opportunities were followed then men and women would be better able to understand the privilege that is involved in being a churchwarden and, at the same time, feel better able, as a result of their preparation and the grace of God, to fulfil it.

When all is said and done, any human being is unworthy of the calling of God in Christ, yet by his enabling we are given strength to fulfil God's purpose for our lives. As God calls so he equips. He will not fail us or forsake us when we offer our lives to him in the service of his Church nor when he calls us to that responsibility through the choice of others.

Appendix
CANON E1 OF CHURCHWARDENS

1. The churchwardens of parishes and districts shall be chosen in accordance with the Churchwardens Measure and any other Measure, Act or scheme affecting churchwardens.

   (a) At a time and place to be appointed by the bishop annually, being on a date not later than 31 July in each year, each person chosen for the office of churchwarden shall appear before the bishop, or his substitute duly appointed, and be admitted to the office ofchurchwarden after –

      i) making a declaration in the presence of the bishop or his substitute, that he will faithfully and diligently perform the duties of his office; and

      ii) subscribing a declaration to that effect and also that he is not disqualified under section 2 (1), (2) or (3) of the Churchwardens Measure 2001.

   (b) In relation to a filling of a casual vacancy the reference in paragraph (a) above to the 31 July shall be construed as a reference to a date three months after the person who is to fill the vacancy is chosen or the date of the next annual meeting of the parishioners to elect churchwardens, whichever is the earlier.

2. Subject to any provision of any Measure, Act or scheme relating to the resignation or vacation of their office, the churchwardens so chosen and admitted shall continue in their office until they, or others, as their successors, be admitted in like manner by the bishop or his substitute duly appointed or, if no person is admitted by 31 July in the year in question, until that date.

3. The churchwardens when admitted are officers of the bishop. They shall discharge such duties as are by law and custom assigned to them; they shall be foremost in representing the laity and in co-operating with the incumbent; they shall use their best endeavours by example and precept to encourage the parishioners in the practice of true religion and to promote unity and peace among them. They shall also maintain order and decency in the church and churchyard, especially during the time of divine service.

4. In the churchwardens is vested the property in the plate, ornaments, and other movable goods of the church, and they shall keep an inventory thereof which they shall revise from time to time as occasion may require. On going out of office they shall duly deliver to their successors any goods of the church remaining in their hands together with the said inventory, which shall be checked by their successors.

5. In this Canon 'bishop' means the bishop of the diocese concerned.

CANON E2 OF SIDESMEN OR ASSISTANTS TO THE CHURCHWARDENS

1. The sidesmen of the parish shall be appointed by the annual parochial church meeting or, if need arises between annual parochial church meetings, by the parochial church council.

2. No person whose name is not on the church electoral roll is eligible as a sidesman, but all persons whose names are on the roll are so eligible.

3. It shall be the duty of the sidesmen to promote the cause of true religion in the parish and to assist the churchwardens in the discharge of their duties in maintaining order and decency in the church and churchyard, especially during the time of divine service.

Useful supporting publications

These books are primarily for reference and should be kept in a place to which church officers have access. The cost of purchase is a legitimate charge on parish funds.

General

A Handbook for Churchwardens and Parochial Church Councillors, Mowbray

A Guide to Church Inspection and Repair
Church House Publishing

How to Look After Your Church
Church House Publishing

The Churchwarden's Year – A calendar of church maintenance
Church House Publishing

Safe and Sound? – A guide to church security
Church House Publishing

The Churchyards Handbook
Church House Publishing

A Guide to the Photography of Church Furnishings
Church House Publishing

Making Changes to a Listed Church
The General Synod

Legislation

The Churchwardens Measure 2001
HMSO

Care of Churches and Ecclesiastical Jurisdiction Measure, 1991
HMSO

Church Representation Rules
Church House Publishing

The Canons of the Church of England
Church House Publishing

Codes of Practice
Care of Churches and Ecclesiastical Jurisdiction Measure
Church House Publishing

Patronage (Benefices) Measure 1986 – Exercise of Rights of Presentation, available from Church House Publishing:

Church House Bookshop
31 Great Smith Street
London SW1P 3BN
Telephone: 020 7898 1300
Fax: 020 7898 1305
Email: bookshop@c-of-e.org.uk
Website: www.chbookshop.co.uk

The Church House Bookshop also operates a mail order service.

Glossary of terms

Archdeacon: an ordained minister, appointed by a diocesan bishop and given responsibility for churches, clergy and churchwardens within an archdeaconry.

Benefice: the living and property attached to a church office, especially that of a rector or vicar.

Bishop: a diocesan bishop is a person who has been consecrated a bishop and given responsibility for a diocese. An area or suffragan bishop is given a share in the responsibility of a diocesan bishop.

Chancellor (of the diocese): the chief officer and judge of the ecclesiastical court of a diocese.

Collation: the admission to office of an ordained minister when that office is in the gift of the diocesan bishop.

Deanery: a collection of parishes under the responsibility of a rural or area dean.

Diocese: a defined geographical area of parishes under the pastoral responsibility of a diocesan bishop.

Electoral roll: the list of qualified ecclesiastical electors within a parish.

Faculty: the legal permission authorising a parish to carry out work to the fabric or contents of its church building or within its churchyard.

Institution: the admission to office of an ordained minister when that office is in the gift of an individual or group other than the diocesan bishop.

Interregnum or vacancy: the period when there is an interval in the normal ordained ministerial leadership in a parish.

Inventory: a list of all articles belonging to a church.

Licensing: the occasion when an ordained minister or lay person is given the diocesan bishop's licence to carry out particular responsibilities and tasks.

Logbook: this contains a full note of all alterations, additions and repairs to a church, the land and other articles belonging to it.

Parish/parochial: a geographical area having an ordained minister and designated place of worship licensed to it by the diocesan bishop.

Patron: a person or group having the right to present an ordained minister to a benefice for licensing by the bishop.

Plurality: more than one benefice.

Presentation (suspension of): the situation which exists when a diocesan bishop suspends a patron's right of presentation.

Quinquennial inspection/report: a report on the fabric of a church produced on a five yearly basis by its inspecting architect.

Rural/area dean: the person given responsibility for a collection of parishes by a diocesan bishop.

Sequestrator: a person given legal responsibility for the care of a parish during an interregnum/vacancy.

Service register: the register in which are recorded details of services held in a church or designated place of worship.

Synod (General): the body of bishops, clergy and lay people chosen to represent the dioceses at national level, meeting for consultation and decision making.

Synod (Deanery): the body of elected clergy and lay people within a deanery meeting for consultation and decision making.

Terrier: a list of all lands belonging to a church.

Visitation: an official visit and inspection made by a diocesan bishop or archdeacon within their area of responsibility.